As Above

Also by Christine Quintana

Selfie

Espejos: Clean (adapted and translated into Spanish by Paula Zelaya-Cervantes)

As Above

Christine Quintana

Playwrights Canada Press
Toronto

First edition: October 2025
Printed and bound in Canada by Imprimerie Gauvin Ltée, Gatineau

Jacket art and design by Katie So
Author photo by Sally Zori

Playwrights Canada Press
202-269 Richmond St. W., Toronto, ON M5V 1X1
416.703.0013 | info@playwrightscanada.com | www.playwrightscanada.com

LIBRARY AND ARCHIVES CANADA CATALOGUING IN PUBLICATION
Title: As above / Christine Quintana.
Names: Quintana, Christine, author.
Identifiers: Canadiana (print) 20250196166 | Canadiana (ebook) 20250199742 | ISBN 9780369105820 (softcover) | ISBN 9780369105844 (EPUB) | ISBN 9780369105837 (PDF)
Subjects: LCGFT: Drama.
Classification: LCC PS8633.U5835 A91 2025 | DDC C812/.6—dc23

Playwrights Canada Press staff work across Turtle Island, on Treaty 13 and Treaty 20 territories, as well as unceded lands, which are the current, ancestral, and future homes of the Anishinaabe Nations (Ojibwe / Chippewa, Odawa, Potawatomi, Algonquin, Saulteaux, Nipissing, and Mississauga / Michi Saagiig), the Wendat, members of the Haudenosaunee Confederacy (Mohawk, Oneida, Onondaga, Cayuga, Seneca, and Tuscarora), and the xʷməθkʷəy̓əm (Musqueam), Sḵwx̱wú7mesh (Squamish), and səlilwətaɬ (Tsleil-Waututh) Nations, as well as Metis and Inuit peoples. It always was and always will be Indigenous land.

We acknowledge the financial support of the Canada Council for the Arts, the Ontario Arts Council (OAC), Ontario Creates, the Government of Ontario, and the Government of Canada for our publishing activities.

Canada Council for the Arts | Conseil des arts du Canada
ONTARIO ARTS COUNCIL
CONSEIL DES ARTS DE L'ONTARIO
an Ontario government agency
un organisme du gouvernement de l'Ontario
ONTARIO CREATES | ONTARIO CRÉATIF
Canada
Ontario

To my mom, my grandma, and my aunt;
my roots, my trunk, my branches.

This play was written on the ancestral lands of the Musqueam, Squamish, and Tsleil-Waututh Nations; of the Lekwungen peoples, also known as the Esquimalt and Songhees Nations; and on Treaty 7 territory. No gratitude is enough for what these lands have given me.

Foreword

Tasha Faye Evans

Have you ever loved a tree? Stood raptured in a magnificence that is both tree and more than tree? All at once calm, any dis-ease gently realigning into place? I am often moved to tears in the presence of trees, particularly old-growth Cedar trees—*Thuja plicata* of the *Cupressaceae* species.

Of the many discussions I had with Christine Quintana about *As Above*, I was most impacted by our conversations about well-being and how central the land, particularly a tree, is in the telling of her story. I was struck by Christine's hesitance to centre Cedar in her story, as if a Douglas Fir or a Willow might be more respectful to write into her play as a settler in these Coast Salish lands and waters. When we talked about her own personal healing, it was indeed a Cedar tree she had loved because that's what Cedars do. Here on the Pacific West Coast, a Cedar is understood as the Tree of Life. Their roots weave baskets to cradle newborns while their highest branches once held loved ones on their way to the spirit world. A Cedar's inner bark, its phloem, is woven into clothes, baskets, hats, and mats. Carved into canoes and house posts, Cedars provide transportation and shelter. Cedar is danced in ceremony, worn as regalia, carved into masks, rattles, and drums. Perhaps most significantly in the context of *As Above*, for all our relations, Cedars cleanse. They give fresh air and their boughs wipe our spirit clean. Some call Cedars grandmothers, mother trees, matriarchs of these lands. Others remember that Cedar is monoecious, both male and female. When we give thanks, we raise our hands like Cedar boughs, swaying softly in the wind. I raise my hands to Christine for the subtle and beautifully complex ways she has found to weave Cedar tree medicine so respectfully into her storytelling.

I was taught that Cedars grow a root above ground for children to sit and listen to stories. Have you ever climbed into a Cedar's lap and listened to its story? For decades I have walked past a Cedar tree on my way to catch the SkyTrain into Vancouver. Sometimes I stop and pick Cedar boughs to bring into work with me. Most often I will stand under her canopy and just breathe. I feel peace in her presence. She is soft spoken. I call her aunty and thank her for the life she breathes into me. I am always relieved to see her on my way back from the city, as if she stands there waiting for me to come home.

After the land where she grew was sold to a developer, a fence was built around the neighbourhood. I can no longer walk that way and pass the tree. Every house was emptied and demolished one by one. Even through the fence it is quite satisfying to see how quickly the wild takes over. One Monday morning, I woke up desperately needing to see the tree. I sent an urgent email to the developer asking for access to the site. I wanted to say goodbye. I waited all day for a reply until I finally decided to just go to the gate and ask to be let in. But as I got there I discovered I was too late. All the trees had been felled. In one day a whole neighbourhood forest had been reduced to a field of stumps. Massive piles of branches and broken trees spread across the horizon. I wanted to fall to my knees, and I could have if I wasn't caught by the most enchanting smell. A thick Cedar sweetness hung heavy in the air as if the tree herself had called to say, "Come! Remember me this way."

Colonization disrupts the original relationship with these lands and all our relations. I am grateful for the truth *As Above* teaches about heartache, the debilitating dis-ease knowing the earth is more than a resource, that a tree is more than a tree, that winning doesn't always look like winning when we fight for what we believe. A Knowledge Keeper can point out the medicines of all the indigenous plants growing in the forest, reminding us that every species has its own gift to bring to the world. *As Above* invites us to not underestimate the relationships we make with the land. May we remember that just as each plant grows with a purpose, so do we, and when we walk, the earth rises to hold us beneath our feet.

Tasha Faye Evans is a Coast Salish dance and theatre artist, educator, and consultant. Her body of work is an intersection of artistic practice, culture, and education woven into dance and theatre performances, city-wide cultural reclamation projects, and innovative curriculum. With decades of creation and production, Tasha has participated in performances and festivals nationally and internationally. https://tashafayeevans.com/

Foreword

Allen Larocque

At the core of their essence trees are no different than us. We are cousins in the phylogenetic tree of life, each of us an outgrowth of the singular genetic seedling that sprouted early in Earth's history and has since been branching its way through the ages. If this were a song every branch of life would be a genre, every species a theme, and every individual a variation.

Like us, trees have parents, children, brothers, and sisters. They have neighbours and neighbourhoods. They have friends and enemies. They eat food and are eaten in turn (an experience fortunately rare for humans these days!). Trees breathe in and breathe out; they thirst and sip water; they transpire just as we perspire. Like us they are conceived, born, and die.

On the surface there are differences, too. Our favourite modalities of communication are sight and sound. But plants have no eyes to see with and no ears with which to hear. They are instead chemical creatures, their leaves attuned to the taste of signalling molecules in the air and their root tips to the flavours of moist soil underground. Here it is dark and quiet. Here fungal threads carry chemicals along highways created by their reticulated, networked bodies. Like our nerves, electrochemical action potentials ripple along the outside of their chitinous sheaths, relaying messages we are just beginning to understand. These messages seep from fungi to plant roots through structures called mycorrhiza, structures that are neither plant nor fungi but somehow both, an intimate mutualism between fungal thread and plant cell.

Where there is message there is response, and where there is response there is communication. This is simply cause and effect. These effects trigger a chemical cascade that results in behavioural change in the plants, and these changes are physically preserved in the flesh and wood of the individual tree. These individuals in turn interact, and these interactions become preserved in ecological patterns in the forest. Through this emergent encoding action thus becomes memory. These patterns connect us to each other both in the present and through time in ways that we are not aware of, in ways that are deep and dark. It is these "connections between" that separates the forest from the trees. This is the difference between a group of individuals and a community.

Like our communities, forests are not so much something to be understood as something to be *in relationship with*. Western science has long approached forests as something *out there*, something primarily to be *understood* and *managed*. We know, deep down, that this is wrong: we know that approaching our personal relationships the same way does some kind of violence to the other. It boxes our relations in, it reduces them to our *idea* of them rather than seeing them for what they *really are*.

Like a loved one we seek to understand forests, but we never quite get there. Something always escapes us; they are always just a *little bigger* than our conceptions of them. They are always growing and changing, and our ideas are, at best, always a few steps behind. They are deeply *weird*, in the terminology of ecologist Timothy Morton. In their strangeness they are both comfortable and mysterious, both healing and frightening, simultaneously familiarly close and incomprehensibly distant.

The longest and most stable relationships are the ones that seek to preserve this *weirdness*, this wonder and mystery: when the person you wake up next to every day surprises you, when the person you see in the mirror every morning is somehow different, when the tree you walk past every day catches the light in a way you've never seen before. In these moments we are reminded that we are not just ourselves, but all our relations, too. The connections *are* us, whether we want them to be or not.

Dr. Allen Larocque is a forest ecologist, forester, and data analyst living in Vancouver, British Columbia. His Ph.D. work examined how mycorrhizal networks distribute nutrients from dead salmon along salmon streams. He currently works for the Canadian Forest Service.

Foreword

Meg Roe

One of the intricately woven themes Christine Quintana wrestles with in *As Above* is the familiar, deep pull of intuition. At the centre of the play we watch Jo, a deeply sensitive, fiercely intelligent woman on the search for redemption, or forgiveness, or maybe just peace. Jo has this *feeling*, this niggling, persistent feeling that someone is reaching out, that something is communicating. She can't shake it; she sees evidence all around her, and she finds herself chasing its meaning, desperate to understand the message.

I think we all understand that feeling that something is calling to us. It's hard to say whether this voice is supernatural, but it can certainly feel that way. It's a voice I've heard when I've been close to illness, to babies, to death. That little feeling you get just before you lose something. That tiny voice just before you knock a jar off a counter. The instinct you get to look up just in time to see your kid do something magical. A knowing: this baby is going to be born today. That feeling: she will not survive this. It's familiar. It happens all the time, is known. It can be hard to listen to, hard to act on. For me, it's louder in the company of others. It's louder next to water. It's louder in the company of trees.

In *As Above*, and particularly through Jo, Christine suggests intuition is a current, flowing just below the surface, waiting to be tapped. A presence, a phone line, a manifest communication system pulsing around and through Jo, calling out to her. Christine connects intuition to land itself and to the non-human systems operating around us, investigating what it means to be a part of somewhere. Tapped in. A settler on Indigenous territory, a transplant, disconnected from her original soil and replanted into a new and complicated system, Jo is reaching to connect to the place she finds herself living. As a settler myself, what I find so moving and so familiar in *As Above* is the idea that the land and the non-human beings around us are welcoming, ready, and waiting for reciprocity and relationship. That they are indeed reaching out for us, to us, willing to communicate and offering belonging. I am awed by the idea that perhaps intuition is a form of connectivity to everything around us, a matrix of memory and experience, lived by many, many different living things.

I am attracted to this idea of intuition as it relates to theatre and art because, for me, it's what theatre-making is all about. From the very beginning of a process, from the first read of a piece, there is this niggling feeling of How To Do This Play or How This Play Should Feel. The feeling is spontaneous and instinctual and absolutely specific to the artist. It's a little mysterious voice pointing you toward How. You get this idea of where to start, and then the rest of the process is all about trusting and listening, like plugging in the right cables to get to the real message. Theatre is about connection and relationship and communication and all the same things we're looking for in life, and in creating it you're always in dialogue with the mysterious voice, with your intuition.

The funny thing is that, often, rather than just listening and following the message we're receiving, we try to shape it, or corral it into something understandable, tangible, controllable. This is true for me in my work and in my life. It's probably true for most of us. A kind of doubt seeps in. Perhaps because it can be hard to admit that we might be held by something larger, or that we're an integral part of something delicate and massive, surrounded by pulsating mycorrhizal tendrils. Maybe.

Really, I'm attracted to the idea of intuition because it feels like a guide to living well. Not just art-making or not dropping the jar or looking up in time to catch your toddler's eye. Late in the play we discover that the someone who is communicating with Jo might just be Jo herself, some deep knowledge inside her, calling out for attention and care. Or maybe it's all the same thing: the supernatural is us, the banal is the divine, the earth and the land and even one another all sending the information we'll need to make things beautiful and to make beautiful things.

JO: AND NOW I'M THE SUGAR AND THE SAP
AND THE SALMON BONES IN THE ROOTS AND THE
MEMORIES IN THE HEARTWOOD I AM
EVERYTHING NOW
BECAUSE SHE IS HERE

AND I DON'T HAVE TO UNDERSTAND IT
I JUST HAVE TO LET GO

Meg Roe is a Canadian actor, director, composer, sound designer, and dramaturg whose work has been seen and heard internationally on both stage and screen.

As Above was first produced by the Belfry Theatre, Victoria, from February 6 to March 3, 2024, with the following cast and creative team:

Gabrielle Rose: Jo
Hrothgar Mathews: Rick
Sereana Malani: Everyone else
Christine Quintana: Standby, Everyone else

Meg Roe: Director
Camellia Koo: Set Designer
Stephanie Kong: Costume Designer
John Webber: Lighting Designer
Alessandro Juliani: Composer & Sound Designer
Emily Cooper: Projection Designer
Tasha Faye Evans: Cultural Dramaturg
Treena Stubel: Intimacy Director
Caryn Fehr: Stage Manager
Becca Jorgensen: Assistant Stage Manager

Characters

JO: fiercely intelligent, tremendous capacity for error
RICK: salt of the earth, kind heart, dark side
A third actor plays everyone else

Notes

Slashes (/) indicate the spot where the next line should begin.
[Brackets] are what the character stops themselves from saying.

Winter

Somewhere.

JO: There is this small glade of trees near my apartment, just down the road.
I used to stop there on my way home.
There is one tree in particular, much older than the rest.
I used to visit it often.

At night, when I couldn't stand to be alone, I would walk down and lie next to the trunk, in the dirt, in the moss
And I would rest.
I would imagine the fungal networks snaking up the cuff of my pants, climbing into my shirtsleeves
Curling around my ribs
Breaking me down
And returning me to the earth
To be in service to this tree.

Every day, then, felt like an eternity, every dry hour, every aching second
And I thought, what does it matter?
Here I am
Prostrate in the presence of the oldest living beings on earth
What does it matter if I stay
What does it matter if I go
Just let me go.

But the earth never wanted to take me.
So I would dust myself off and go home.
Alone.

JO is at a restaurant with RICK. A server is standing over their table.

SERVER: And have we decided on drinks?

A brief pause.

RICK: Not yet, thanks.

SERVER: No worries, I'll give you a moment to think.

The server leaves.

JO: I don't drink.

RICK: I know. Me neither.

JO: You know?

RICK: Your necklace—I saw your necklace in your picture/ it's a—

JO: / Oh, right

RICK: —so I figured—

JO: Right. Well done. It was just a birthday gift from my sister. Haven't worn it since.

RICK: I—sorry, I didn't mean to make you uncomfortable.

JO: You haven't.

RICK: Good.

JO: And I saw on your um, profile. "One Day At A Time."

RICK: Yeah. My experience so far has told me that people can be very uh, what's the word—shitty.

JO laughs and is surprised that he made her laugh. RICK is pleased.

Shitty, there's my elegant way of saying it. So I've figured it's easier to just put it out there.

JO: Maybe.

RICK: I thought that's what you were doing with the *(gestures to her necklace, which she is not currently wearing)* the necklace, in the picture.

JO: No, just thought it was a nice picture.

RICK: It is.

JO: And nice, I guess, not to have to explain.

RICK: Exactly.

JO: Eight years.

RICK: Twenty-seven.

The server re-enters.

SERVER: All right, any decisions made?

JO: I'll get a cranberry juice with soda water, please.

RICK: Water's fine for me.

SERVER: Great. Shall I take these drink menus away, then?

JO & RICK: Yes.

In a greenhouse, JO *is addressing a small crowd of people.*

JO: Hello everyone—anyone who's here for the workshop, please gather 'round to where you can hear me. Thank you.

Hello everyone, welcome, and thank you for being here today for our talk, "#PlantsMakeEverythingBetter." My name is Dr. Joanne Heywood, and I'm part of the staff here at the Gardens. It's important to acknowledge, as we do, that today we are standing on the traditional, ancestral territories of the Lekwungen peoples, also known as the Esquimalt and Songhees Nations. These are the original caretakers of this land who, frankly, did a hell of a lot better job than we're doing right now. In my experience, this is true all over the world. I've had the privilege of visiting and conducting research in places where Indigenous knowledge about land stewardship is being reclaimed after centuries of erasure under colonial rule, which did not value or understand that knowledge.

Today, most of the plants that surround us here at the gardens are not indigenous to this territory. Like myself and perhaps most of us here today, many of these plants are growing far from their native land. Some have been traded, captured, accidentally transplanted, taken far from their place of origin, grown and cultivated in greenhouses many generations over, and now captured in the frame of your iPhone lens. The popular hashtag "plants make everything better" doesn't begin to describe the knowledge and richness plants have to give to us.

So, let's dive in.

JO *is being examined by a* DOCTOR. JO *is already pulling up the side of her shirt before the* DOCTOR *says:*

DOCTOR: All right, let's take a look—great, all right then—

JO: / See?

DOCTOR: / Ooh, ouch, yes that looks painful.

JO: And it just showed up, out of/ nowhere, I just woke up and—

DOCTOR: / Do you remember scratching? In your sleep?

JO: No, I was asleep, so / I wouldn't remember scratching even if I—

DOCTOR: / It looks like irritation from bedbug bites.

JO: Bedbugs? No—

DOCTOR: I'm afraid so.

> *The* DOCTOR *is already writing a prescription, not exactly listening anymore.*

JO: No, I definitely don't have bedbugs.

DOCTOR: No one ever wants to have bedbugs, but in my experience that is always what it turns out to be.

JO: I just don't think / that's what it is, it feels like something else.

DOCTOR: / But, you should know that bedbugs have nothing to do with cleanliness or sanitation, it just happens. The bus, maybe a friend's couch, who knows. But the bites can be quite itchy, so you were probably just scratching yourself at night.

JO: Okay.

DOCTOR: I'm giving you a prescription for Betamethasone—just a topical cream to help with the itching.

The DOCTOR hands JO the prescription and moves toward the door without stopping.

JO: All right, / but should I come back if something—

DOCTOR: Have a good day, take care.

JO is at home, talking on the phone with her sister HAZEL, trying desperately not to scratch.

JO: That's what I'm saying, Hazel, I don't think he listened to me at all—

HAZEL: They never do, they make money per patient, you know.

JO: Oh, I didn't know that.

HAZEL: Yeah, it sounds like your clinic just tries to pack in as many people as possible.
And besides, wouldn't you rather have a female doctor? / I sure would.

JO: / I don't really care.

HAZEL: This is why I'm telling you, you should find a GP that's accepting new patients—

JO: Do you know how long the wait lists are here?

HAZEL: It's no better in Calgary.

JO: I told you, I appreciate it but I'm fine.

HAZEL: When was your last mammogram?

JO: Oh for god's sake Hazel, you sound just like Mum.

HAZEL: No, really.

JO: You know, I have no idea.

HAZEL: No idea like five years, or no idea like never had one?

JO: It hasn't exactly been top of mind.

HAZEL: It never is, but it should be—at our age / we need to be thinking ahe—

JO: Oh for god's sake, that's enough. Jeeeeeesus.

HAZEL: I'm just saying.

JO: *(teasing, kindly but annoyed)* I'm just saying.

HAZEL: Oh that's real mature, aren't you supposed to be the big sister?

JO stops.

JO: Oh, shit—

HAZEL: What?

JO: I bled through my shirt.

RICK and JO's second date. They're walking with coffees.

JO: I googled you.

RICK: Uh oh.

JO: Par for the course, just making sure you weren't a felon or, I don't know.

RICK: Fair enough. What'd you find out?

JO: I saw that CBC story.

RICK: Right.

JO: About your business.

RICK: Yeah.

JO: You're nice. You're very nice.

RICK: Well, I don't know. It just made sense.

JO: Uh huh.

RICK: My team is usually about six or seven guys, and I'd been working with this one guy, Khaled, for about five years, and I was so wrapped up in my own stuff at the time that I didn't even really register that when I heard him talking on the phone with his family, he was speaking Arabic. But when all the Syrians started showing up, I was thinking man, I wanna do something and then bam, I just realized I could, you know?

JO: "Looking Out."

RICK: Yeah, that's what my brother Tobey used to say all the time. So that's what I renamed my contracting company—well you read the article, so. Anyway yeah, Khaled translates, runs the crews, and they work in Arabic and start learning English as they go. Khaled's family is from Jordan, so his dialect is a bit different but we make it work together. Get these newcomers working and making money and feeling good here. We have twenty guys now, we're pretty busy. I'm grateful for it.

JO: You're very nice.

RICK: I have a lot to make up for.

JO: Sure. But you're also very nice. You'll have to forgive my suspicions.

RICK: Of course you're suspicious, in your line of work. Plants. Nasty buggers. Mean spirited!

JO: Oh, you have no idea.

RICK: I gotta admit, I don't actually know what ecologists do.

JO: Neither do we.

RICK laughs gently. JO hesitates.

I used to teach at UBC but I uh, don't now. I was doing research there too. About uh, a decade ago. I didn't work for a few years. Now I'm at the botanical gardens.

RICK: That's great!

JO: It's good.

RICK: Sometimes "good" is good enough.

JO: That's what I've been telling myself.

RICK: I'm not kidding though.

JO: Me neither. I have "sometimes good is good enough" embroidered in cross-stitch above my toilet.

A moment passes. RICK looks at JO.

What?

RICK: I don't really do banter. You're good at it and I find you very funny and charming but I don't really banter. It's fun for a while but it doesn't really interest me as much as saying what I really mean. I think we might be able to relate to each other in a certain way, but only if that's what you're looking for.

I don't mean to be so blunt, but I just don't want to waste your time, or mine.

JO: Okay.

They stand for a moment.

Well.
I have a thirty-three-year-old daughter I haven't spoken to in nine years.
My husband died of prostate cancer ten years ago, but I was an active alcoholic at the time and couldn't even drive him to doctors' appointments or the hospital.
I managed to lose tenure status shortly after that.
I go to AA but only once a week and I don't sponsor anyone.
I work a job alongside the people who would have been my students ten years ago.
You're the only man I messaged back on that fucking app and I don't really know what I'm doing or what my intentions are.
There.
Okay?

RICK: Okay.

JO is on the phone with her sister.

JO: So the first complaint was from a woman who didn't appreciate having a land acknowledgement as part of the workshop

HAZEL: Jeez, makes me embarrassed for our generation.

JO: She felt it was "tangential and inappropriate."

HAZEL: Oh sure.

JO: But then, but THEN! They got a second complaint from a young woman who felt this thing that I said about the migration of plant species was "insensitive and colonially violent."

HAZEL: Oh.

JO: I mean I don't know, but it certainly makes me glad not to be in academia anymore.

HAZEL: Are you in trouble?

JO: I think they evened each other out, so they don't really know what to—

JO stops talking and is suddenly feeling sick to her stomach.

HAZEL: Oh, hello, are you there?

JO: Yes, but I—I have to go—

HAZEL: Are you okay—

JO drops her phone and throws up.

JO is at a coffee shop with RICK.

JO: Sorry, I didn't know who else to—
I didn't want to alarm anyone, but I knew that you—

RICK: No, I'm glad you reached out. Happy to help.

JO: Thanks.

RICK: So, what's happening for you right now?

JO: I feel hungover.

RICK: Okay.

JO: But I'm not.

RICK: Okay.

Pause.

You didn't call your sponsor?

JO: I didn't want to—I feel like she'd—no, I didn't.

RICK: And you just feel hungover?

JO: Yes.

Beat.

RICK: It's
If something happened
Anything can be overcome.

JO: No, I didn't
I didn't.

RICK: Okay

JO: That's what's so—
I didn't.
But the feeling is exactly as if I did.

RICK: As if you had a drink?

JO: Yes.
It's just very visceral.

RICK: I bet. I don't miss those mornings.

JO: No, neither do I, which is why this is so disturbing.

RICK: I bet it is.
So how do you feel, though? Right now?

JO: What do you mean?

RICK: What does this bring up for you?

JO: I don't know.

RICK: Do you want to talk?

JO: . . . about? Isn't that what we're doing?

RICK: In a way yes, but

JO: I guess I don't know what I'm asking for

RICK: All right

JO: Look I don't want you to feel like you're at a meeting right now

RICK: Well I'm drinking out of a real mug, for starts

JO: Haha.

RICK: I've had enough of Styrofoam for a lifetime

JO: Me too

Beat.

RICK: I can imagine how scared you must feel right now.

JO: Not scared, but
Uh

Yeah, scared.

Beat.

RICK: This is a moment to call on your higher power.

JO: Look Rick, I'm not really into that [shit].

RICK: It doesn't have to be God, or—

JO: Yes I've heard that disclaimer too, but no thank you.

RICK: All right. Okay.

Beat.

JO: I really don't know why I made you come here. I'm sorry.

RICK: Sometimes it's just nice not to be alone.

JO gives him a quick smile.

So what do you think it is that's making you feel crappy, most likely? Bad piece of beef?

JO: Ugh.

RICK: Expired milk in your morning coffee? Maybe some botulism mixed with dehumanizing shame?

JO: This is helping. I think.

RICK: Why don't we go for a walk?

The greenhouse, JO *is addressing a small crowd of people.*

JO: So. Why is your eighty-dollar *Monstera* dying slowly in your living room? Why is your adorable *Pilea peperomioides* dropping leaves on your windowsill?

Where these plants live in the wild, they are part of complex ecosystems that provide everything they need—water from rainfall, nutrients from the leaves, and droppings of their plant and animal neighbours, the exact weather systems they were meant to live in.

Take them away from those ecosystems, and it's up to you to recreate it as best you can—your success is a matter of life and death.

JO *is on the bus, standing.*

A young woman is sitting nearby, looking out the window. JO *stares at her, as if she knows her.*

The woman turns her head.

WOMAN: Oh, I'm so sorry, here—do you want my seat?

JO: Oh, no.

WOMAN: No please, that was rude of me, I'm sorry I didn't see you before—

JO: No, you just reminded me of

WOMAN: There you go!

JO: I don't need it, I'm not [old]

WOMAN: No, no I know you're not.
You're like the same age as my mom!

JO: Oh great.

JO is on the phone with her sister.

HAZEL: Nothing? No word?

JO: Nothing.

HAZEL: Asshole.

JO: Let's not—

HAZEL: No, let's! Asshole!

JO: Look, I called him in a panic telling him I thought I had a phantom hangover.
He thinks I'm nuts. Or rather—he *knows* I'm nuts.

HAZEL: Still, that's no reason.

JO: Sure, well, that was three weeks ago and I've heard nothing from him, so. Oh well.

HAZEL: I'm sorry.

JO: Yeah. Well. I'll put a homing device on the next one before I spill my deepest darkest fears to a near-stranger. He'll never get awaaaaaayyyy . . .

JO laughs, forced.

HAZEL: Jo.

JO: What?

HAZEL: It's okay to feel hurt.

JO: I don't.

HAZEL: Uh, okay.

JO: Do I feel rejected? Sure.
Betrayed? Perhaps.
Do I feel like . . . a hag? Absolutely.

HAZEL: Oh my god, STOP! It's okay to be hurt.

JO: I've been hurt. This isn't it.

HAZEL: Okay.

A little silence.

JO: I just hoped . . .
Yeah. I just hoped.

HAZEL: I know.

A beep.

HAZEL: Are you getting a call, or am I?

JO: It's me I think.

She looks at her phone.

. . . it's Rick.

A coffee shop.

RICK: So.

JO: So.

RICK: I think I owe you an explanation.

JO: You don't.

RICK: I . . . don't?

JO: Sorry, I sort of interrupted you.

RICK: Okay.

A beat as RICK recollects himself.

I owe—I uh feel I owe you an explanation. For disappearing.

JO: I didn't think I'd hear from you again.

RICK: No, it wasn't
There was no lack of

Hmm.

RICK drinks his coffee, nervous. He looks into his cup. He speaks carefully.

I live with clinical depression.
I have
I have a psychologist, who I see every week
I'm on medication
I do all of the, you know, things you are supposed to do
But sometimes
Despite my best efforts
I go somewhere that's hard to come back from.
I would like to be better
Better at communicating that
But once I'm there I'm sort of
There

Does that make sense?

JO: Yes.

RICK: Okay then. That's uh—that's it.

JO: I was very good, just now.

RICK looks up.

RICK: How uh—what?

JO: You said, "I live with depression" and I wanted to say, "Who doesn't!"
You said, "I go somewhere that's hard to come back from" and I wanted to say, "Like IKEA on a Saturday?"
No banter.
See?

RICK: Yeah.

He looks back at his cup.

JO: Rick.
It's okay.
You're okay.
Thank you for telling me.

RICK: Yeah.
Sure.

JO: How are you feeling now?

RICK: Not quite ready, I think.

JO: Ready for?

RICK: To be

He gestures generally to being out and about.

JO: Thank you, then. For this.

He nods.

They're quiet for a bit. JO *doesn't know what to do for him. She just starts talking.*

I like how you said that.
"Going somewhere that's hard to come back from."

I don't know where I've been.

When I look back at my life
I can't remember anything except for what was right in front of me.
I went to school, I got excited about studying and researching.

I met my husband
We had our daughter
I was working all the time
Somewhere in there I just

I came away from myself. Like the inner and outer part of me just pulled away from each other. There's a haze, on the lens, when I try to see it. I remember it like it happened to someone else. Maybe it was the booze, sure, but there's some other—some other quality. It's hard to say. I was tired, all the time. Overexposed, maybe. So I retreated into myself in a way that I think, at least for a time, was undetectable to everyone else. I was sending my stunt double out while I stayed at home. I remember it for the first time, when I was holding her. Ada. I saw myself in the mirror and my heart stopped for a moment because I thought, who is holding the baby? I forgot where I was. Or who. Or something. That was the first tear in the fabric. It just kept splitting and splitting.

I don't think I know where I've been for the last forty years. And now I'm here. Like, really here. They don't really warn you about that part. It's like when you get a new prescription on your glasses and suddenly the world is too clear. Gross. I don't think I ever wanted to be this alive, and now that I am I don't quite know what to do. Now when I catch a look in the mirror there is no mistaking that yes this is me and I am here and this is now. It's too much.

RICK is now just watching her.

I'm saying this
Ah
I'm monologuing
Because I want you to feel okay.
All this to say
You're definitely not going to be able to scare me
Even if you have to go away, sometimes.

They sit for a while.

RICK: I'm here.
I'm here now.

JO is at the DOCTOR's office. The DOCTOR is examining her.

JO: I just feel like something isn't right.

DOCTOR: Of course.

JO: I trust my intuition.

DOCTOR: Mmmhmm.

JO: And you said to come back if anything changes.

DOCTOR: Absolutely

JO: I'm not a hypochondriac, it's just—ouch.

DOCTOR: Did that hurt?

JO: It's more—uh—tenderness.

DOCTOR: When I do this?

JO: Ouch—yes, that.

DOCTOR: Well that was your back.

JO: Sure.

DOCTOR: Before you said it was your stomach. / Any changes to diet?

JO: / Well, I have felt nauseous—sorry / what was that?

DOCTOR: / any changes to diet?

JO: Sorry?

DOCTOR: Any changes to diet?

JO: No.

DOCTOR: Vomiting?

JO: Well, once / but

DOCTOR: / Perhaps you threw out your back vomiting.

JO: Perhaps.

DOCTOR: Any problems sleeping?

JO: Yes, actually.

DOCTOR: Any changes at work?

JO: No, not uh / really.

DOCTOR: / Lifestyle changes?

JO: Well I started seeing someone.

DOCTOR: Are you sexually active?

JO: Not uh—not yet, I mean it's a little early.

DOCTOR: Do you meditate?

JO: Do I what?

DOCTOR: Meditate.

JO: Absolutely not.

DOCTOR: You should try it.

JO: . . .

DOCTOR: I think most of your symptoms just point to anxiety.

JO: Really.

DOCTOR: Loss of sleep, some stomach upset, you've got some changes to lifestyle.

JO: I just feel like something isn't right.

DOCTOR: Headspace is a great app. Insight Timer, too. In the App Store.

JO: Sure.

DOCTOR: And keep drinking water.

As he's walking out the door:

Let me know if anything changes!

DOCTOR is gone.

JO: I don't want to fucking meditate.

JO and RICK are walking together in a park.

JO: I can't believe I am walking here, in public, being seen with / one of Victoria's

RICK: / Oh stop

JO: Citizens of the Year

RICK: Don't stop

JO: A model Samaritan

RICK: I mean it is an honour

JO: Yes, it is! You were up there with teenagers who saved toddlers from drowning in ravines and police dogs who rescued old ladies. I was very proud.

RICK: You were?

JO: Absolutely.

RICK: Thank you. Khaled looked pretty damn good too.

JO: He sure did but we're talking about you right now. Did you get a medal or something?

RICK: I got a ribbon and a sizable Tim Hortons gift card.

JO: Even better.

RICK: I'd say so.

JO: Your brother would be very proud.

RICK: Yes, I think so.

JO: I'm glad I could come.

RICK: Me too. Glad I could steal you from the *Gladioli. Gladiolus. Gladioluses.*

JO: We're changing over for the spring right now so there's a lot to do.

RICK: You know I've never been to the gardens? I would love to see you doing what you do.

JO: Well

RICK: ?

JO: It's not exactly
It's a change of pace, I guess.

RICK: From the university days?

JO: Yeah.

Well.
It's different.
Humbling.
Which is part of the process, I guess.

RICK: It sure is.

JO: I lived in Bolivia, for a year. For a research expedition. Internationally funded. Back when Ada was little. My husband, Tom, came with me too, worked as my assistant. Which was funny.

We lived in this little house on the outskirts of town. We all drove together with our research assistants in this busted up Jeep into the site. I'd work away, Tom would record our findings, Ada would just wander through the trees, looking at the sky. I worked with Marta Quispe, a very renowned Indigenous conservation scientist. She was so—well, she was very important. I was honoured to work with her.

I was a big deal, once upon a time. Just so you know.

JO stops for a moment.

You know, I think it will be more fun when we get past the exposition part of this relationship.

RICK: I'm interested.

JO: Interested in hearing about my dead husband?

RICK: Whatever, are you interested in hearing about my dead brother?

JO: Jesus, aren't we romantic.

RICK: Look, you should just feel lucky to be walking with me. I've got a ribbon and enough plastic in my pocket for about fifty double-doubles.

JO laughs and takes his arm. It's unexpectedly intimate.

So what are these guys doing?

JO: Who?

RICK: These fellas over here— *(gestures to a bank of trees)*

JO: Oh, the trees!
Well
They're talking.

RICK: Talking?

JO: Of course. I mean, this is of course a heavily urbanized ecosystem, but still.

RICK: How?

JO: They use fungal networks, mycorrhizal fungal networks to communicate, to warn against pests or other invasive presences in the forest, to share sugar and carbon. Think of it as like the internet, or electricity. Or something. They call it the "Wood Wide Web." All thanks to fungus.

Actually, you have a very fungal quality to you, yourself.

RICK: That's normally not a compliment.

JO: It is to me. It's astonishing, really. The deep, deep reciprocity of these relationships. The trees are able to share resources, share knowledge, because of the mycorrhizal networks. Even between tree species, if you can believe it—birch and fir, alders and pine. The fungus facilitates the exchange of necessary goods for living, and in return the network thrives. All this, and then the city plants a single juvenile oak in the middle of a field and wonders why it barely grows. Meanwhile six inches below ground in an established forest, is a complex community of care and exchange that no urban planner could ever recreate.

RICK is looking at her.

What? What?

He kisses her.

RICK's home. They're making out. It's headed somewhere. JO is alternately turned on and uncomfortable, and though she tries to hide it, RICK is observant.

RICK: Is this okay?

JO answers him with a kiss—yes. They make out more. As RICK heads down her body, JO stares off into the distance.

RICK: I, uh—time out.

JO: "Time out?"

RICK: You don't seem uh
Talk to me.

JO: I just haven't done this in a while

RICK: Yeah, me too

JO: Sober.
I haven't done this sober.

RICK: Right.

They part for a moment.

It's harder

JO: Yeah

RICK: Well, different

JO: Very different

RICK: We can stop

JO: No

RICK: Okay

She reaches for him, but he slows her down, gently touching her arms and collarbone.

Let's just take it slow, okay?

JO: K.

RICK: You just have to be here. Like, actually, fully here.

They sit for a moment, maybe looking at each other, maybe not. Very slowly, very gently, he runs his fingers through her hair. She breathes.

RICK: Okay?

JO: Okay.

Spring

JO is giving a lecture at the garden.

JO: Hello and welcome, everyone. I'm so grateful you've chosen to spend your afternoon with us here at the gardens learning a little bit about the incredible trees we have here. As we emerge from the winter months and signs of life are returning to the world around us, I would like to begin this session by acknowledging that we are living here on the traditional, ancestral territories of the Lekwungen peoples, also known as the Esquimalt and Songhees Nations.

I am told that my ancestors were farmers—who knew all about the plants and soil and the rhythms of their own lands back home. And when they and other European settlers arrived here, they brought their own crops, turnips, and potatoes. They did their best to mould the land into something familiar.

The settlers weren't the first to farm these lands. Not even close. The Indigenous people here already knew how to farm the camas and chocolate lily, planted in tandem with the Garry oaks which anchored the soil without shading out the food-giving plants and berries.

But all of that became nearly impossible after the settlers clearcut these areas and drained the wetlands in order to homogenize the landscapes and impose their own agricultural methods. Goodbye berry gardens and chocolate lilies. Hello turnips.

While you are here today to hear me speak, what you should be listening to is the land. I can tell you that time and time again in scientific fields like mine, academic research often merely confirms traditional Indigenous ways of knowing.

In part when we do these land acknowledgements, what we are talking about is respect for this knowledge, which comes from the land itself. An acknowledgement of what has been lost.

Yes, question?

The washrooms are to through the lobby to the left.

Well, let's begin.

JO is on the phone with her sister.

HAZEL: What?

JO: Yes. Meditation.

HAZEL: That's ridiculous.

JO: I did feel very . . .

HAZEL: Patronized?

JO: Dismissed, but patronized fits the bill too.

HAZEL: I think you should get a second opinion.

JO: No, it's okay.

HAZEL: I worry.

JO: You always worry.

HAZEL: Well. [You've given me plenty to worry about.]

JO: Yes, okay. [You win.]

HAZEL: You're not going to, are you?

JO: No. Probably just some light food poisoning or, you know. Whatever.

HAZEL: Whatever you say.

A little pause. Maybe HAZEL *is washing dishes or something.*

I'm good, by the way.

JO: Oh good.

HAZEL: Thank you for asking.

JO: I didn't.

HAZEL: I know, I just thought I'd, you know, enjoy the fantasy

JO: Sorry!

HAZEL: Of my attentive and considerate sister

JO: Sorry! You are good?

HAZEL: Who always asks me, how are you, how was your day?

JO: All right, all right.

HAZEL: I'm reading a great book.

JO: That's great.

HAZEL: Jer and Gav are going away for the weekend so I get to look after Priya.

JO: Oh, fun!

HAZEL: You should come visit.

JO: I would love to.

HAZEL: You would love to but

JO: I would love to but I can't.

HAZEL: You would love to but you can't because?

JO: I don't have the money, Hazel.

HAZEL: Right.

A brief pause in which everyone knows what's coming.

They speak simultaneously.

HAZEL: / Let me buy you a plane ticket.

JO: / I would love to see you but I'm not taking a plane ticket.

HAZEL: Why not?

JO: Because

HAZEL: Because why? Don't be stubborn.

JO: Don't be pushy.

HAZEL: I'm not being pushy!

JO: I'm not being stubborn, I'm saying no thank you.

HAZEL: I want to see you but also you need a little break, you've been sounding—

JO: What?

HAZEL: —I don't know
A little
You could use a change of scenery.

JO: Well, I'm going away this weekend.

HAZEL: You are?

JO: Yes.

HAZEL: Where?

JO: Uh, out to Cowichan Lake.

HAZEL: Just by yourself?

JO: No. Rick invited me.

> *HAZEL holds the phone away from her and reacts ecstatically; JO rolls her eyes knowing what's probably happening.*

HAZEL: That's great.

JO: I don't know what I'm doing.

HAZEL: You're going on a weekend getaway with a man you're interested in.

JO: Ugh.

HAZEL: What?

JO: I don't know.

HAZEL: It'll be nice.

JO: Yes.

HAZEL: You can have nice things. You deserve nice things.

JO: Sure.
Anyway . . .

How's your book?

JO and RICK are driving toward the cabin. JO has her head swaddled in a scarf, crumpled in the passenger seat.

JO: Car sick. Like a two-year-old, or an elderly beagle.

RICK: It's fine. The Malahat is the world's best free rollercoaster. Wheeee!

JO: Ha ha.

RICK: We're almost there.

JO: You've been saying we were "almost there" since I vomited into your water bottle.

RICK: Let's just forget that ever happened, but we really are almost there. In fact.

He takes a turn. We hear the crunch of gravel, and the engine turns off.

Ta daaa.

JO moans and unwraps her head, takes a moment to get her bearings. Then:

JO: Oh my god.

RICK: No need to oversell it / it's just a modest—

JO: / No no no I mean I know this place. I know . . .

She gets out of the car and immediately kneels on the ground, placing her hands on the earth.

RICK: You uh—you've been here?
Jo?

She walks to a tree and touches the trunk.

She reacts like she got an electric shock, and her hands shake.

I feel like I'm interrupting something here.

Slowly, she places her hands back on the trunk.

It might take JO some time to answer him.

JO: Yes. I grew up here.
Practically
Uh
This cabin belonged to my family. Four generations.

RICK: Are you serious?

JO: After my parents passed, Tom and I bought my sister out and it was mine.
Ours.
I lost it, when things
When things

You bought this in what, 2014?

RICK: Yeah.

JO: You bought this land from me.

RICK: Holy shit.

JO: Yeah.

RICK: That's incredible. Absolutely incredible.

Beat.

Higher power?

JO: Coincidence, Rick. But a good one. I never thought I'd see this place again.

RICK: I bet.

JO: Let me show you around.

JO and RICK are at the cabin, sitting on deck chairs watching the water.

JO: It's a beautiful morning.

RICK: yeah

JO: Coffee, sweater, thick socks.

RICK: Uh huh.

JO: It's the life.

RICK: Yep.

JO: It's so beautiful here.

RICK: . . . [you don't have to comment on everything.]

JO: What?

RICK: Listen . . . shhh . . .

They listen to the silence of the early morning. JO *does her best, then starts to shift uncomfortably.*

JO: Look at the fucking sunrise.

RICK: I did.

JO: And you look fantastic.

RICK: Thanks

JO: Your arms, my god. Do you work out?

RICK: I'm a contractor, Jo.

JO: Right, well

RICK: . . .

JO: Birds. I don't hear anything but birds, no traffic, no voices—

RICK: You can hear the birds, eh?

JO: Right. Right. Sorry.

A pause.

Do you feel that? That cool breeze? That's not the water, you know, that's the trees.
Even though it's been so hot. Too hot.
Did you know these are some of the oldest trees in the world? Maybe not these ones right around here, but in this area. It's astonishing, really.
You see all that footage on the news of those trucks coming down the highway with those massive, massive—
I mean maybe at that point it's considered "lumber"
I find that offensive
Because you look at those trees, the width, the *age*
That's not industry
That's
That's something else.
Cathedrals.
That's what they call those places, where the old giants are together.

RICK: Cathedrals, eh?

JO: Yes.

RICK: Hmm.

> *JO sits with this for second. She thinks about the feeling of being back with the cedar, with the lake, with the trees. She's quiet for a moment. Then:*

JO: Sometimes I [wonder about how our lack of connection to nature is the worst poison in the world, worse than alcohol, and I wish all of us could spend more time outdoors and maybe then we'd finally have a chance to heal.]

You know, when I touched that tree [I got the clearest feeling of being connected to something beyond myself that I've ever experienced.]

> *Pause.*

RICK: Hmm?

JO: No, nothing.
Sshhh, listen
Birds.

Nighttime. The cabin. It's well after dinner, they're playing cards and laughing hard. We don't know what they were laughing at, but it's been a good, long, deep laugh for them both.

JO: *(wiping tears from her eyes)* Oh god.

RICK: That was a good one.

JO: It sure was.

She sighs deeply. They settle, maybe with a few last simmers of laughter. RICK looks at JO.

What?

RICK smiles.

Did I pee myself? What? What are you looking at?

RICK: You.

JO: Yeah?

RICK: Yeah, you.

JO holds his gaze, looking back at him.

I feel like I know you.

JO: I don't know how to tell you this, but . . . you do.

RICK: No, I mean
Like I've *known* you.

JO: Biblically?

RICK knows now to wait her out, until she's done making jokes.

Yeah
I didn't think I liked people anymore
But you
You are one of a kind.

RICK: Thanks. You're all right.

JO starts crying again.

JO: Oh no.

RICK: What is it this time? Am I too handsome? Too funny? I can tone it down, I promise.

JO keeps crying, turns away. He gives her space. She moves away from him.

JO: It's all so
It's hard for me to describe what it's like to be back here
I just feel like I've changed so much but this
Uh
It's like this place remembers
It's just
There's no way I can atone for
Every little thing I've rebuilt
feels so, so delicate
temporary
Like someone
some*thing*

is going to come by, and they're going to say "oh no, not you—you shouldn't have been given this, this is not for you"
this deep dread
I'm sorry

RICK: It's all right.

JO: Sometimes I get this flash
like I'm cheating on Tom
I'm with you and I think what am I doing
what am I doing

You know, cedars are different

The beech and the fir trees use ectomycorrhizal networks, they go wide and far, but the cedars use arbuscular mycorrhizae—you're glazing over—

RICK: No, no I'm listening, I'm listening

JO: The cedar's networks go right into their own roots. They stay close. Tight.
That's how I thought of us. Just the three of us against the world.
Me and Tom and Ada.
And we were all here, together
He proposed to me under the tree out front.

He said he had hoped he would get to die here, but we never made it back after he got really—
And now here I am with you
it's like I forget
because I was so, so fucked up
when he died, all of it

it's like there's a missing reel or something
I forget

I forget everything.

RICK: That's shame.

JO: What?

RICK: Shame. That's shame.

JO: Yes.
Shame.

They sit.

RICK: Be careful with that one
I'm not telling you you can't feel what you feel but
Shame's powerful.
I know it well.

We used to swim in this lake when we were kids, me and Tobey
He was a much better person than me.
But I'm the one still here.
I'm not much of a swimmer, now.

What good is that?

JO: I'm sorry, Rick.

They sit, with this. It's not entirely clear what this means. Gently, RICK maybe gets up and tidies something.

JO sits.

The phone rings, loud.

(startled) Jesus Christ.

RICK: That's odd.

JO: Landline?

RICK: Yes, but I never—

He picks it up.

Hello?
Sorry, I can't really
Hello?
Yes, can you hear me?
Who?
Sorry—
Yes.
She's here.

He holds the phone out to JO.

It's for you?

JO: Me? Who is it

RICK: I don't / know, she sounds very

JO: How do they know I'm here

RICK: I don't know, I just think you should—

She takes it

JO: Hello?

She's listening, stunned

Ada?

Honey, is that you—
Yes, I'm okay, are you
I can't hear you
What's wrong?
Where are you?
Ada?
Can you hear me?
Can you hear—
Hello?
Hello?
Ada?

She hangs up. She looks at RICK.

RICK: What was that?

JO: I think that was my daughter—

JO anxiously paces the cabin, on the phone with HAZEL.

HAZEL: Okay, slow down, I'm trying to catch up here—

JO: Bolivia

HAZEL: What?

JO: The phone number traced to an area code in Bolivia / but when I called back

HAZEL: / Did you call back, or—

JO: Nothing, it didn't even ring, I just got a—a—message in Spanish, and

HAZEL: Okay

JO: Do you know where she is?

HAZEL: Jo.

JO: I'm not accusing you, I'm not angry, I just need to know if you know where she is.

HAZEL: No. I would have told you / if I knew anything

JO: Then how did she find me?

HAZEL: I don't know, maybe she remembered the landline number and thought she'd try you there, she doesn't know that you lost—that it's not yours anymore

JO: Goddamnit.

HAZEL: Just stay calm

JO: How am I supposed to stay calm?!

HAZEL: I know it must be unsettling

JO: Yes it's fucking unsettling.

A pause.

You haven't talked to her?

HAZEL: No.

Beat.

Not in years, she uh

JO: What?

HAZEL: She cut me off too.

JO is in alone in bed, trying to sleep. She breathes deeply. It doesn't work.

She gets up, pours a glass of water. Takes a sip. She sits down on the edge of her bed. She is anxious, upset, grieving. It shows.

She stands up to get back in bed and suddenly clutches her stomach, in tremendous pain. She cries out.

Summer

JO is on the phone with HAZEL.

JO: That doesn't make any sense

HAZEL: I told you everything I know

JO: Okay.

HAZEL: You can believe me, or not, but / I'm telling you the truth

JO: / I believe you, it's just —

HAZEL: What?

JO: I don't know. I don't know.

HAZEL: You don't know how much it all hurt me.

JO: Trust me, I can understand—

HAZEL: Well no, not quite. Because I didn't do anything wrong.

A pause.

JO: Right.

HAZEL: I was only trying to help.

JO: So she was in Montreal, at McGill

HAZEL: Yes

JO: What was she studying?

HAZEL: Ecology.

JO: Until when?

HAZEL: Five years ago.

JO: And then?

HAZEL: That's when she cut me off.

JO: Why?

HAZEL: I wanted her to invite you to her graduation ceremony. I thought it would be a good way to reconnect, you were doing so well. I pushed her too hard. She cut me off. I went to the ceremony but she stopped contacting me after that.

JO: And you didn't do anything?

HAZEL: I've tried. Her friends will confirm that she's safe, that she stayed in Montreal after graduating. But that's it. I haven't heard from anyone in about a year and a half now. But I feel confident that her friends would have reached out if anything had happened.

JO: Jesus Christ.

HAZEL: What?

JO: You never thought about telling me any of this information?

HAZEL: For you to do what? I only managed to keep in touch with her on the condition that we never talked about you, and I wasn't to tell you anything about her. I just wanted to keep her in my life, to let her know she was loved / and wanted

JO: / by someone who wasn't a fuck-up.

HAZEL: Look, Joanne.

JO: Oh, look out, we're on full-name basis now.

HAZEL: I did my best under excruciating circumstances.

JO: "Excruciating!"

HAZEL: Don't do this. Don't get mean.

JO: And what exactly do you characterize as "mean"?

HAZEL: Look, I've been patient. Very very patient.

JO: I'm going to hang up now.

HAZEL: Don't hang up on me.

JO: Fine.

Beat.

HAZEL: Wow. Is this growth?

JO: You tell me.

HAZEL: You do get mean, you know.

JO: I know.

I just.
I am not equipped, for this.

HAZEL: What do you mean?

JO: It's too much. Knowing my baby is out there, and something could be wrong, and I can't do anything, and my fucking body is falling apart, and I can't do anything for her or myself or anyone else.

HAZEL: No one is equipped for something like this.

JO: I don't think that's true.

HAZEL: What is it you think anyone else has that you don't?

JO: Look at our family, Hazel. We have no traditions, no religion, no customs or rituals, or anything. Not even clogs at Christmas.

HAZEL: What do clogs have to do with anything?

JO: We have nothing left of—of—people are supposed to—I mean who knows, maybe that's why I used to drink. We're supposed to have these things that guide us, that give us some kind of shape to life to help us get through moments like these. Without it, you just spend your whole life reaching. You just end up one of those old white ladies with a dreamcatcher in the window and a Buddha statue in your garden.

HAZEL: Jo.

JO: We have nothing. Our ancestors gave us nothing.

HAZEL: They gave us a cabin.

JO: I don't think we're talking about the same thing.

HAZEL: If you say so.

Beat.

JO: Do you remember that big tree, out front of the cabin?

HAZEL: The Dougie?

JO: It's a cedar.

HAZEL: Sure, yes. Anyway, of course I remember, why?

JO: I
Nothing.

Beat.

Bolivia. I'm not surprised Ada wanted to go back.

She loved the trees, and the warm weather. She loved Marta and her son, so much.
We were so happy, there.
I think that's the last time we were.

HAZEL: Are you all right?

JO: I'm fine I'm just lost
I'm lost.

The DOCTOR's office, again. The DOCTOR examines JO's abdomen.

JO: No.

DOCTOR: No change in diet?

JO: No.

DOCTOR: Any unusual exercise, stretching, exertion?

JO: No.

DOCTOR: Anything else to report?

JO: I'm uh recently sexually active.

DOCTOR: Good for you. Discomfort is not unusual in this case.

JO: Look, I *know* something is not right, and I don't appreciate—

JO goes to stand. She cries out and collapses.

JO is at home, in bed. RICK has a large tote bag full of items.

RICK: Thanks for inviting me over. Letting me look after you a bit.

JO give a thumbs-up.

I didn't think that uh fashion magazines were your thing so
National Geographic
Maclean's
A *National Post*, real print newspaper, how novel eh?
And also some snacks
Chocolate, some fancy crackers and cheese
This really good sausage from the market
Uh
A candle?
It smells good. To me. I think.
A lighter! For the candle.
Yes.
And me.
Until you tell me to go away.

JO smiles.

Does that mean go away?

She shakes her head.

How bad is it right now? The pain.

She holds up seven fingers.

Seven?
Out of five?
My god!

She drops six fingers, leaving only her middle finger. She smiles. RICK laughs.

I'm sorry you're hurting so much.
Have you tried meditation?

JO: Fuck you.

RICK: There she is.

A wave of pain. JO closes her eyes.

They didn't give you anything at the ER?

JO: They offered, but I said no.
Codeine.

RICK: Ah

JO: Yeah.
Not worth the risk.

RICK: Right.

You're tough, Jo. You can do this. But you should have stayed at the ER—

JO: I waited six hours, I think they forgot I was there. I'd rather be at home with sausage and *Maclean's*.

RICK: I do what I can.

She exhales deeply as the pain passes.

JO: Where is she
That's all I can think about.
Where is she?
Why is she calling now?
No more calls from that line?

RICK: I've been checking, nothing.

JO: But how? And why now?
What can I do?

RICK: Right now, you need to rest and take care of yourself—

JO: That's what I've been DOING
I need to DO SOMETHING but I don't know what
What if she's in trouble?
What if she's scared?

RICK: But first you need to rest. You need to care for yourself.

JO: You said that already

RICK: Well you didn't listen.

A wave of pain. JO breathes deeply.

Listen. I want to pray for you.

Pause.

JO: Pray for me?

RICK: Yes. If you're comfortable with it, I would like to do that for you.

JO: For me?

RICK: Yes.

JO: Are you sure it would be for me?

RICK: I
Well
I guess it would be for me as well, if that's what you mean.

JO: Well, it would only be for you, because it wouldn't mean anything to me.

Beat.

RICK: All right.
It's all right if you're not comfortable. I understand.
But I need you to understand that my faith is important to me, and it's not something I take lightly. I'd ask that you not take it lightly either.

JO: Look, I hear what you're saying, but / I don't have the capacity to have a theological discussion with you

RICK: / As soon as you come in with the "but" it makes me think that you don't hear what I'm saying—

JO: I am dealing with a *real crisis* that is *actually happening around me* right now, and I don't have it in me to argue about prayer or higher powers, or whatever—

RICK: —sorry I asked.

Beat.

JO: Look, don't make me the bad guy now. You asked me if I was comfortable, I told you no / and now I'm getting guilt / tripped

RICK: / Actually you didn't say no, but— / oh come on, no one is guilting you.

JO: But that's what it's about, isn't it? Guilt? Surrendering to some higher power because we are just guilty pieces of shit who have more apologies to give than we have years left on earth? They lost me at Step Two. I'm supposed to believe that some "higher power" that allows the shit that goes on in this world is going to "restore me to sanity"?

RICK: All right, that's enough.

JO: What more do you need, Rick? Everyone knows how good you are, you pray, you show off your virtue with your fucking company /

RICK: / careful, there

JO: / you're Mr. AA and that doesn't change a thing that's already happened. You said it yourself, that you have a lot to make up for. If you want to pray, pray, but just admit that it's only to make yourself feel better. Nothing else.

Beat.

RICK: I'm going to go now.

JO: Okay.

RICK: We don't have to talk about what just happened.
You seem very sure of yourself, so there's not much more to say.
You're in pain, Jo.
You're in pain.

He leaves.

JO and HAZEL are at JO's apartment.

JO: I wish you'd let me know you were coming, Hazel, I don't really have / any

HAZEL: / The couch is fine.

JO: I don't even have / enough pillows.

HAZEL: / It's fine, Jo.

JO: Okay.

A pause.

Why are you here?

HAZEL: I just thought, with your health, and this strange situation with Ada, and your little blowout with Rick, that you could use a little company.

JO: Okay. And you didn't let me know this because?

HAZEL: Because I knew you'd tell me not to come.

JO: Okay.

HAZEL: I'm worried about you.

A long pause. HAZEL sits down.

Tell me the truth.
If you've been drinking, you have to tell me.

JO: I haven't

HAZEL: DON'T lie to me, do not lie about this.

JO: Honest to god, Hazel, I / have been sober this whole time.

HAZEL: / because I can't—I mean I will, but you can't put me through this again.

JO: What again?

HAZEL: The lying. Picking fights for no good reason. Insane [fucking] behaviour. You can't put me through this again.

JO: Oh for god's sake.

HAZEL: Just when we spoke, and you said you felt "lost."
It just made me feel [frightened]

HAZEL takes a moment and squares herself.

I think you've relapsed.

JO: There it is, I knew it was coming, I knew you'd get there eventually. You don't trust me.

HAZEL: Trust you? And what could possibly make you think I can trust you?

JO: I have worked hard for eight years / to try to make up for

HAZEL: / And you think eight years will do it? For forty years of being put through hell by you? For sitting in fucking hospice care with your husband while you were passed out drunk on your kitchen floor?

JO: I don't need this right now.

HAZEL: Sure you never need it, there's never a good time, there's never a right way to have this conversation with you.
Don't you dare judge me for how I've chosen to handle what you've put me through. Don't you fucking dare.

HAZEL's cellphone rings. JO is eerily, intensely focused on the phone.

JO: Answer it.

HAZEL: We are in the middle of—

JO: Answer it.

HAZEL: I don't even recognize this number—

JO: Just answer it.

HAZEL does.

HAZEL: Hello?
Hi, sorry, who?

(to JO) They're speaking Spanish, I don't—

JO: Give it to me
Hola
Soy Joanne Heywood, la hermana de Hazel
Lo siento, hablas inglés?
Okay.

(aside to HAZEL) They're calling from Bolivia.

(back to phone) Esta bien, puedo entender un poco
Lento, lento por favor
Sí, ella es mi hija
What? She what?

When—perdón—cuando (ah fuck) cuando salió? When did she leave?
Okay.
Claro.
Como encontrar mi hermana?
Claro.
Muchas, muchas gracias.
Adios. Bye.

She hangs up.

HAZEL: What happened?

JO: Ada was at a research centre in La Paz. She left two days ago without telling anyone. You were her emergency contact.

HAZEL: Oh my god.

JO: Look I told you, I fucking told you—

JO winces with pain. The wind picks up.

JO is pacing, leaving a voicemail for RICK.

JO: Hi Rick, it's me. I just got off the phone with the embassy—it took some convincing but they did tell me that Ada got a Bolivian visa in August of last year—it's still in effect so odds are she is still there. I'm betting anything she went back to the area where we did our residency—I don't know, I'm grasping at straws here.

I know I owe you an apology. I'll make it a good one, I promise. Please call me back. I just want to know you're okay.

JO is at the DOCTOR's office. She is in so much pain, she is almost short of breath. The sound of rain, outside.

JO: Look, I don't want to be here again, but I can't wait three months for a CT scan, and if you don't help me I'm going to go to the critical care clinic / or, or emergency AGAIN, or—

DOCTOR: / That won't be necessary, and according to my notes you did refuse treatment at the ER—

JO: I didn't "refuse treatment," I went home because I was hungry and tired / and hurting

DOCTOR: / I think the CT will bring you some peace of mind.

JO: "Peace of mind?"

DOCTOR: There's no need to get upset, Ms. Heywood.

JO: Don't do that, don't patronize me again, *please.*

DOCTOR: Would you like me to just speak frankly then?

JO: I am begging you to do so.

DOCTOR: Look. You are getting older. There will be changes in your body that take some time to adjust to. You can't come in here every time something new comes up.

JO: That's not what this is.

DOCTOR: And there's another factor.

JO: Yes?

DOCTOR: You're an addict.

Pause

JO: I've been in recovery for eight years.

DOCTOR: If the CT does show something, we might be looking at something like cirrhosis.

JO: Ah. Something that's my fault, then.

DOCTOR: That's not what I said. But likely, it's nothing. Or nothing serious.

JO: So it's all in my head then?

DOCTOR: Sometimes the emotional pain that addicts previously treated with alcohol or drugs manifests in other ways, sometimes.

JO: Psychosomatic.
So you think I'm crazy.

DOCTOR: Not at all. I just—

JO's phone rings.

JO: Oh shit, sorry

Hello? Oh my god—shit, yes, I'm on my way. I'll be there in twenty. So sorry. Be right there.

JO is lecturing at the garden, not at her most "in the zone." Heavy rain pounds on the glass of the greenhouse roof.

JO: Hello everyone. These gardens sit on the ancestral territories of the Lekwungen peoples, also known as the Esquimalt and Songhees Nations. I've been asked to scale back my land acknowledgements, in response to a letter in which a garden visitor said they felt "shamed," to which I say you are grossly overestimating the utility of your shame. Who asked for it? Not me. Not the dozens of First Nations communities without clean drinking water. So if you're feeling ashamed, do something about it and please write a letter to Mr. Carney, not to me.

Where were we?

Ah yes, we are here today to talk about fungi, which are more than just good in salads, or fun for recreational use!

Mycorrhizal networks are critical to the information infrastructure of forests or gardens. For example—say a tree is being attacked by pine beetles. Even though it may be too late for that particular tree, she will send an alert—an alarm—through the mycorrhizal network, a warning to her fellow trees. Even without ever encountering the predator, a neighbouring tree can then go into emergency response mode, producing the necessary chemicals needed to keep them safe, long before . . . Excuse me . . .

> *JO is outside her apartment, pacing, leaving a message for RICK. She is nervously rubbing her stomach, unconsciously. The wind and rain are relentless.*

JO: Hi, Rick, um
I realize this sounds insane but I don't know who else would maybe understand but
If all this stuff happening to me isn't real
According to my doctor, Hazel, and whoever else has an opinion about me
Then maybe it's something else
I think
I think maybe
I think Ada is calling me
Maybe
I think she needs me

I don't
I can't explain it
It's just
I had scratch marks and no bed bugs, I had abdominal pain with no discernable health issues except being an old fucking addict,
I was hungover
without drinking
Maybe it's because we

At the cabin, the tree
When I touched it I just got this feeling
This—I don't know
I felt something.

And then she calls, and then she disappears
And all these things that are going on
I just
I think that we're connected

I just have this feeling that something is wrong
And she's calling me
She needs me
And maybe this is
I don't know
my uh [higher power]
But um
Are you okay?

A huge crack of thunder.

JO is at RICK's office, waiting, anxious. The radio plays in the background.

CBC: Power outages, fallen trees, and structural damage. These are just a few of the things Victoria residents face, as a powerful storm in the midst of the driest summer on record tears through Vancouver Island. CBC is on the scene in Sooke, where trees of up to twenty metres in height have toppled, leaving massive root structures on display, and neighbours fearing for their safety. We spoke to—

KHALED enters, a man in his late thirties, energetic with an easy smile. JO startles, as if she sees something, or someone else.

KHALED: Hi there—

JO: Oh—uh. Hi there—uh—Khaled?

KHALED: Yeah that's me, how can I help you ma'am?

He turns down the radio.

JO: I don't know if you remember, we met briefly at the Citizens of the Year / Awards thing

KHALED: Oh, Jo, hi! Nice to see you!
Rick talks about you like, all the time.

JO: Oh, I don't know if— He does?

KHALED: Oh yeah.

JO: I really need to talk to him
He's not answering my calls, or anything—

KHALED: Right.

JO: You haven't talked to him?

KHALED: He hasn't been in. We've agreed that I just keep things going when he's not here.

JO: Okay.

KHALED: I'm sure everything's all right.

JO: We had a
we had a fight
I just feel like I
Um

A flash of lightning. JO *startles.* KHALED *sees that she's distressed.*

KHALED: I can maybe let him know you came by

JO: So you are talking to him?

KHALED: Well
I don't know what you want me to say.

JO: So he's talking to you but not me?

KHALED: I think he needs space, is all. And it's also one of those . . . one of those times.

JO: Right.
I don't think I realized you two were close.

KHALED: Of course.
I mean
Yeah.
I assume everyone has a certain idea of what this company is
But it's not that, you know?
We're like brothers.
So [I'm not going to bother him]

JO: Right.

Well, I won't take up any more of your—

JO winces suddenly as pain shoots through her abdomen.

KHALED: Are you okay?

HAZEL is in JO's apartment.

HAZEL: So here I've made a list of all the flights from La Paz to Montreal, and to Vancouver for the last three days.
Her friend Natalie last talked to her four days ago at the research centre, so she couldn't have left before that.
I've made a list here of all the possible connections, and I'm using Skyscanner to check them off as they go.
That's about as far as I can go for now, but it will give us a bit of sense of when
If she's coming.

JO: You think she'd go back to Montreal?

HAZEL: I don't know
I'm grasping at straws here, I just feel like I should do
I don't know, something
how are you feeling?

JO: Tired, really tired.

HAZEL: Yeah, I bet.

JO: Do you want some tea?

HAZEL: No thank you, I'm all right—wait I don't know why I said that, just habit I guess.

Yes, I'd like tea.

JO puts the kettle on, and as she does so she watches her sister, who looks over her handiwork but mostly sits, very tired as well. She comes back and sits with HAZEL.

JO: We're not young, are we?

HAZEL: Wow, not sure where you've been the last few decades, but no we're not.

JO: It just hits me sometimes.

HAZEL: Yeah.
Yeah.

JO: I'm glad you're here.

It's a tough moment.

HAZEL: Terrifying, terrifying
I don't have the words to describe how absolutely
Horror
It's horror
Watching everything unfold and feeling so so helpless
I'm sorry for doubting you, it's just
If you had been through what I went through

JO: I understand

Beat. HAZEL starts for the kitchen.

HAZEL: Well, the tea is probably ready.

JO: Oh god, maybe we're British.

HAZEL: What?

JO: Come here.

HAZEL faces her.

I love you.

HAZEL: I love you.

There's a knock on the door. JO immediately tenses.

Who is that?

JO: I don't know.

HAZEL: Easy, Jo, it could be anything.

JO: Okay. Okay.

She opens the door. It's RICK.

Oh my god—oh you poor thing, you're soaking wet.

RICK: Yeah, all that just walking from the truck—

JO hugs him, he tentatively hugs her back.

HAZEL: This is Rick?

JO: Yeah.

HAZEL: *(impressed)* Oh, okay.

JO: Rick, this is my sister Hazel.

RICK: It's nice to meet you.

HAZEL: And it's nice to meet you, Jo didn't tell me you were [this handsome]

JO: Easy there, sis.

RICK: I got your text messages Your fifty-two text messages.
You filled my voicemail inbox.

JO: Sorry.

RICK: No it makes sense, communication between a depressive sober alcoholic and a highly neurotic sober genius.

Beat.

I'm assuming she knows everything.
Sisters always know everything.

HAZEL: Yes they certainly do.

JO: Can we have a moment?

HAZEL: Of course, I'll go work on the tea.

HAZEL leaves.

JO: Hi.

RICK: Hi.

JO: Um. I won't waste any time here.
I'm sorry.
I'm very sorry for my behaviour and the things I said.
I really wanted you to just meet the sober, reasonable, decent version of me but the alcoholic is still in there, I guess. Even without the booze.

If there's any mercy it's that this time I can't say I didn't remember, or it wasn't that bad.
I have no right to be resentful of you for having healed your relationships with other human beings.
This is me, owning up.
So.
Yes.
I didn't think I'd ever see you again.

RICK: I would have at least properly dumped you.

JO: Oh fantastic, that's reassuring.

Beat.

RICK: I didn't mean to disappear that completely. I'm not going to pretend our conversation didn't trigger it, but it was [absolutely terrifying]
It was a bad one.

JO: I was scared

RICK: Me too. I uh . . . I can't take another one of those.

JO: Understood.

RICK: But I'm here now.

JO: Thank you. Thank you for coming back.

Beat.

There are things happening right now that I don't know how to explain.

RICK: Yes, you left me a very very long voicemail about it. The trees.
The fungus.

JO: Oh god . . .

She covers her face, embarrassed. He steps forward and holds her.

My fungus. I missed you.

HAZEL walks back in with the tea—sort of awkward because they're having a moment, but too late to turn back.

RICK: I feel like in some way it makes sense.

JO: You do?

RICK: You're
You're picking up signals because you've cleared the channel.

Beat.

Without all [the booze]
That's why
That's why you can hear the signals now.

HAZEL: I like him.

JO: Me too.

The power goes out, and they are plunged into darkness. At the same time:

RICK: / Ah, shit.

JO: / What happened?

HAZEL: / Oh no.

RICK: The storm is pretty bad, we lost power over at the office already too.

JO: Fuck fuck fuck.

HAZEL: It's okay Jo, where do you keep your candles?

JO: I don't know, I don't know / I don't even know if I have

RICK: Over here.

He goes to get candles.

HAZEL: Have a seat Jo, it's okay.

JO: I
I
I

HAZEL: Breathe for me, okay? Take a deep breath.

JO: *(to HAZEL)* Ada

Beat.

HAZEL: It's me, Hazel.

JO: Oh Jesus, I know it's you, I just
I just misspoke.

HAZEL: Okay.

JO: Something's happening
Something's wrong

RICK: Okay, let's get some light over here, we're all good.

JO: Something's wrong

HAZEL: Let's get you that tea, okay.

RICK comes over and is rubbing her back.

RICK: It's okay. It's going to be okay.

JO, suddenly calm, touches his cheek.

JO: What would I do without you?

Beat.

JO is suddenly on high alert, with an unnerving intensity.

Your phone

RICK: What?

JO: Your phone your phone your phone
Check your phone

RICK: What do you mean?

His phone rings.

JO: Pick it up pick it up

RICK: Okay, okay I—
Hello?
Yes, this is he.
No, I'm not there right now.

JO: Someone's there

RICK: *(to phone)* No it's a vacation residence
Maybe the storm, yeah

JO: We have to go

RICK: Jo, honey, just a—
Yes, all good.
No don't send anyone—I'll check it out when I can

JO: We have to go

RICK: Thanks a lot
Bye.

He hangs up.

That was the security company, the alarm went off at my cabin—

Before he's even done speaking, JO *is up and reaching into the pocket of his coat.*

JO: Where are your keys
Do you have enough gas

HAZEL: You can't go anywhere, it's too dangerous right now

JO: What if the highway is blocked
Maybe we'll walk

HAZEL: Cut it out you're scaring me

JO *looks right at* HAZEL.

JO: I'm scared.
I'm scared.

RICK: Jo look at me
Look at me

HAZEL: What should we—

RICK: I don't know, this is—something is wrong

JO: Something's wrong something's wrong something's wrong

She cries out and holds her stomach. She screams in pain, and HAZEL *and* RICK *rush forward to help her.*

The lights come back on.

JO: *(suddenly calm)* We just need to go to the cabin, and everything will be okay.

A huge crack of thunder.

JO *and* RICK *are in* RICK*'s truck.* JO *is now very calm, her intensity completely faded into a focused stillness. The radio signal fades in and out.*

CBC: With over 80% of Vancouver Island and the Sunshine Coast without power, British Columbians are wondering just how long the latest weather incident is going to last. Officials from the Victoria Police are urging residents to stay indoors, closely monitor any flames or candles used for light or heat, and to check on elderly or otherwise vulnerable neighbours.

RICK *turns the radio onto some gentle classical music.*

RICK: I think we've had enough of that.
We're close.
Can't believe none of the highways were closed, that's some good luck, but I'm not sure if we should be out here right now.
I don't think we should stay the night, I think we should go back tonight and see if Hazel has found anything. Maybe when the storm stuff dies down we can go to the police station.

What are you thinking?

JO: Marta.
Marta was like a sister to me.
I don't know if she felt the same, but she was more than a colleague to me.
Watching our kids play soccer in the field
Washing root systems with our bare hands, pointing out things to one another, sitting in the quiet of the forest, bathing our kids in the stream, wiping their hands clean.
Even after the interpreters were done for the day she and I would stay up, patching together our languages, eating food, talking about our children, the forest. Trees. How if we just take care of the land, it will take care of us. She told me about all the work they were doing to protect the land.
How our research would make a difference.
I remember I kept having this feeling, this is it.
We're going to save the world.
(that was back when alcohol still said nice things to me)

Beat.

And then one morning we woke up and they were gone.
Marta, and her son.
She had received a death threat and left overnight.
The interpreters told me she could never come back, or they'd kill her
The thugs that worked for the Canadian mining company that sponsored my wing of the university.
I finished my research there knowing Marta would never see those trees again.
Never see her own land, ever again.
How do you live with that?

RICK: Shit.

JO: What?

RICK: The road is blocked, up ahead.

JO: What do you mean?

RICK: This is as far as we can go
There's a tree—

JO: But we're almost there—

RICK: Look over there, I can't get—

JO: No.

JO opens the door

RICK: Jo—

The quiet of the car gives way to the roar of the storm, the wind whipping through the trees.

JO runs toward the cabin.

Illuminated just by the distant light of Rick's headlights, JO sees a body, lying circled around the trunk of the cedar, facing the tree.

JO stops, cold.

She walks forward slowly.

JO: Ada?

Slowly, ADA lifts her head. She sees JO.

ADA: Mom?

JO: Ada

ADA: Mom.

ADA slowly stands up. She stares at JO.

ADA: I thought you were [dead]

JO: No

They stare at one another.

JO steps forward to embrace her daughter.

JO: Ada

ADA: No, don't

ADA steps back. JO stands still. ADA breathes, heavily. The wind whistles through the trees.

ADA: I hate you I ha—

JO: That's okay

I love you.

ADA stands still, rigid.

Her face falls.

Rain falls on them both.

She reaches for her mother.

JO comes forward and holds her.

ADA: *(whispering)* It hurts

JO: It hurts.
It hurts
It—

Slowly, within ADA's embrace, JO crumples to the ground. ADA catches her, the full weight of her mother in her arms.

ADA: Mom?

ADA is waiting, alone, in the hospital. She looks stone cold, solid. We see her cycle through a few things:

- *i.* *She is texting furiously to someone.*
- *ii.* *She is looking for a piece of gum she knows is somewhere in her bag but she is unable to find.*
- *iii.* *She is staring intently at something we can't see—another patient, or perhaps another person waiting.*
- *iv.* *She is incredibly tired and on the verge of falling asleep.*

After some time, RICK appears with two cups of coffee.

RICK: Sorry, it was a bit of a
Cafeteria just closed.
But there's a machine. Had to find the machine and then find my way back.
I got a latte and a mocha, not sure which one you'd prefer

ADA: I'll take the latte, thanks.

RICK: There you go.

They sit for a bit.

I have a blanket in my trunk, if that might—

ADA: I'm fine, thanks.

RICK: You're soaking wet.

ADA: I'm fine, thanks.

RICK: Sure thing.

A pause.

ADA: You have to understand that I have no idea who you are, okay? I get the sense that you two are in a relationship or whatever, and maybe you know a whole lot about me but I don't know a single thing about you. I understand that you want to be here and you should be here, but the experience I'm having is that I'm sharing this very stressful moment with an absolute stranger, so you're going to need to understand that, okay?

RICK: / Okay.

ADA: / Thank you for the coffee.

At her absolutely stone-cold "thank you," RICK almost chuckles—almost. He surprises himself and stops but not before ADA clocks it.

RICK: You know, you're a lot like [your mother]

He looks away, apologetic. He's tired, not trying to be unkind. But she won't let him get away with it.

ADA: I've been awake for like thirty-seven hours now. If you even so much as imply that I am anything like my mother, I will kill you.

RICK: Luckily, we're in a hospital, so I might survive . . .

ADA: I'll kill you fast, Rick.

They're riding the line of joking and not joking, but ultimately ADA's *threat comes off hilarious. They laugh, giddy with fear and exhaustion. After not too long,* ADA's *laughter starts to change into something else. She might shake, or cry, or be unable to catch her breath.* RICK *is not far behind her but he takes her coffee from her, offers her a tissue from his pocket. He holds the space.*

I can't believe this.
I can't believe this.
I'm not ready.
I'm not ready.
I *just* [went through this]

I had a dream about a fucking tree
How stupid is that
Scared everyone at the centre
My aunt freaked out all my friends, they all thought I was dead too
Because I just got on a plane to come here, didn't tell anyone, just went

I dreamed that the cedar fell down
And if the cedar fell down then that meant

Stupid.

She's driving me fucking nuts
Even now.

RICK: *(very quietly)* Just breathe, Ada.

She breathes and steadies herself, which means she starts to feel it all.

ADA: I am like her.
I am.
I know that.
But I look like my dad.
I hope you see that.
I hope you've seen pictures of him.
It's our eyes.
And our laugh, apparently.
You see a picture of me as a baby and a picture of him as a baby and you couldn't tell us apart.
That always bothered her.
She said it didn't but I know it did.
Because people were always like "you look just like your father"
but she just heard "you look nothing like your mother."
She blew up once, in a playground.
Did she tell you about this?
Yeah, I figured she didn't.
I've just heard parts of this story back, I was too young to remember exactly what happened, but I was playing with my friend Tara and then all of a sudden I hear my mom making a scene, and all the moms are gathering around. I guess Tara's mom had said to my mom "Oh, that's your daughter? I didn't know she was yours." I ran up to her and she was just yelling at this woman, and Tara was crying and holding onto her mom, and I was just standing there feeling like shit, and eventually Dad showed up (which I guess solved the goddamn question for everyone) and tried to get her to calm down and she was like "I'm standing up for our family, Tom, let me do this on my own." and I remember he just said to her very

clearly, "You're scaring our daughter, Jo." Like he was reminding her that I was there. And she turned and looked at me like she'd never seen me before in her life.

And then at the funeral it was just person after person
You look just like your father
You look just like your father
She couldn't look at me.

But the really fucked up thing is
Since then
Since he died
I look more and more like her.
I started to see her everywhere, in everyone all the time
Like, to a weird degree
I literally kept thinking I was seeing her
I mean I wasn't, but
And most of all, I was seeing her in myself.

A pause.

I'm sorry. I'm so tired.
What's happening now?

RICK: All we can do now is wait until she's out of surgery.

ADA: Do they think it's [cancer]

RICK: It's too early to tell.

ADA: Okay.
Okay.

They sit.

RICK: You know, she thought there was something wrong with you. Like all of the symptoms were you calling out to her, for help. She thought it all made sense, the timing of it all.

ADA: Right. Or maybe it just was what it was.

RICK: Sure
But
Can I ask you something?

ADA: Sure.

RICK: How did you know you needed to come?

ADA: I don't know.
I just did.

ADA scratches her side. RICK looks at her.

Fall

Somewhere.

JO: Here, (right here) where we live, the cedar is the tree of life.
I used to romanticize cedar as this mycorrhizal outsider, but that's not so
At least, not in the way I liked to think about it
Cedar is, of course, deeply connected to everything
The First People here use cedar for every aspect of life
You are sent to the spirit world in cedar when you die
You are wrapped in it when you are born.

ADA: I have been grieving my mother since I was born
One day I said goodbye to the mom who smiled in the mornings
Goodbye to the mom who I could trust with my secrets
To the mom who said I love you without wanting something in return.

JO: The roots of a tree are woven tightly with threads of fungus, sewn into the heart of the earth.
Some people assume that the root structure is a mirror of the tree itself.
As above, so below.
It's not. Tree roots are shallow and wide, like the ripples on a pond.

RICK: There was a long time when I believed I wasn't hurting anyone but myself
Pretty silly, eh.
Pretty naive.
Funny how something can be so obvious to everyone else
And completely hidden from you
So you go through life believing you're somehow outside of it all.

ADA: I come halfway across the world for a feeling
And then I'm holding her in the backseat of the car
And she looks so small
She used to take up all the space in the world
And now she's almost whittled down to nothing.

RICK: It's much scarier to know that you're needed
That you need, too.

RICK: The night my brother died, I woke up in a cold sweat		
In the middle of the night, halfway across the country	**ADA:** Holding my mother, I just felt this panic,	
Three time zones away I just knew	She's the only one who remembers Dad What it was like to be us	**JO:** Meanwhile, in the heart of the tree lies a record of everything that ever happened in that forest.
	The beautiful things, and the awful things too	It's seen hundreds of their children live, grow, die, thrive.
I just knew.		
	I don't want to hold it all alone.	
		And these trees remember everything.

RICK: I remember that feeling every time I get close to someone
This invisible thread that ties us together
And I think, can I bear to do this again?

JO: And when they die, the forest and the fungus rush to hold what they can of the wisdom, the life force, of the one no longer alive.

ADA: I can't hold it alone, I don't want to, I can't bear it.

JO: The forest does not want to forget them.

ADA: I just want to start over again with everything I know now.

JO: These giants
These living archives

They're called Mother Trees.

<table>
<tr><td></td><td></td><td>JO: Once I lay at the foot of a cedar tree</td></tr>
<tr><td></td><td>ADA: Mum? Can you hear me?</td><td>And I thought “just let me go”</td></tr>
<tr><td>RICK: But like it or not, we are part of each other</td><td></td><td></td></tr>
<tr><td></td><td>You called me, and I came. I came, Mum.</td><td>And then a fungus came and wove me into the web of everything.</td></tr>
<tr><td>No one gets to count themselves out</td><td></td><td></td></tr>
<tr><td></td><td>Don't leave me now.</td><td>The tree of life.</td></tr>
<tr><td>All you have to do is surrender.</td><td></td><td></td></tr>
</table>

JO: And now I'm the sugar and the sap
and the salmon bones in the roots
and the memories in the heartwood
I am everything now
Because she is here

And I don't have to understand it
I just have to let go.

ADA: Mum?

JO smiles.

Blackout.

Special Thanks

Briony Penn, Allen Larocque, the Mother Tree Project, Angela Roe, Michael Shamata, Sandra Ferens, Scott Bellis, Kayla Dunbar, Jiv Parasram, Molly MacKinnon, James Fagan Tait, Sally Zori, Steph Troughton, Angie Descalzi.

Manhattan Theatre Club Workshop—February 2023: GT Upchurch, David Zayas, Annette O'Toole, Nicole Shalhoub, Laura Smith.

Belfry Theatre Workshop—December 2021: Melissa Oei, Gabrielle Rose, Hrothgar Mathews, Meg Roe, Tasha Faye Evans

Born in Los Angeles to a Mexican American father and a Dutch British Canadian mother, Christine is now a grateful visitor to the unceded lands of the Musqueam, Squamish, and Tsleil-Waututh people. Christine is an actor, playwright, producer, and dramaturg. Nominated for a Governor General's Literary Award and winner of an LA Drama Critics Circle Award, a Dora Mavor Moore Award, a Jessie Richardson Theatre Award, the Tom Hendry Award, and the Siminovitch Protégée Prize, Christine's works have been translated and performed in Spanish, French, German, and ASL in over ten cities worldwide. As a performer, she's acted on stages big and small, in a camper van, in neighbourhoods across East Vancouver, and on a farm. Christine is a graduate of UBC's BFA Acting Program.